NASCAR in the Pits

By Mark Stewart & Mike Kennedy

Lerner Publications Company/Minneapolis

The publisher wishes to thank science teachers Amy K. Tilmont and Jeffrey R. Garside of
the Rumson Country Day School in Rumson, New Jersey, for their help in preparing this book.

Lerner Publications Company
A division of Lerner Publishing Group, Inc.
241 First Avenue North
Minneapolis, MN 55401 U.S.A.

Website address: www.lernerbooks.com

All photos provided by Getty Images.

Library of Congress Cataloging-in-Publication Data

Stewart, Mark, 1960-
NASCAR in the pits/by Mark Stewart & Mike Kennedy.
p. cm. -- (The science of NASCAR)
Includes index.
ISBN 978-0-8225-8738-5 (lib. bdg. : alk. paper)
1. Stock car racing—Juvenile literature. 2. Pit crews—Juvenile literature. 3. Stock cars
(Automobiles)—Maintenance and repair—Juvenile literature. I. Kennedy, Mike (Mike William), 1965-
II. Title.
GV1029.9.S74S748 2008
796.72–dc22   2007028346

Manufactured in the United States of America
1 2 3 4 5 6 – DP – 13 12 11 10 09 08

Contents

Introduction

During a NASCAR race, drivers pass one another at dizzying speeds. But the most important passing doesn't happen on the track. It takes place when the cars are not moving at all—in the pits. Drivers can more easily gain precious seconds with a superfast pit stop than they can by roaring past another car.

This book looks at everything that happens during a pit stop. When a driver pits—and how quickly the pit crew performs—can make the difference between first place and fifteenth place. On most days, less than a lap separates the two results. When pit crew members say every second counts, they really mean it!

TWO CREWS COMPETE FOR PRECIOUS
SECONDS DURING A PIT STOP.

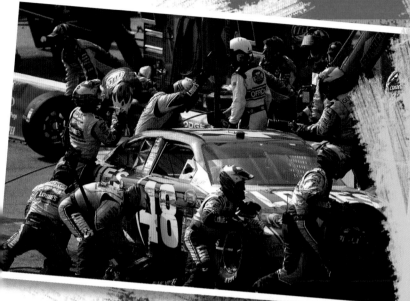

Who's Who in the Pit Crew

Seven members of a racing team make up the pit crew. Only these seven people can hop over the wall that divides the pit area from the track. As fast as they can, the pit crew members put on new tires and pour in more fuel. They also make other necessary adjustments (changes).

Each crew has one jack man, two tire carriers, two tire changers, one gas man, and one catch can man. Men and women do these jobs in a pit crew. The names with "man" in them are left over from the early days of racing. At that time, very few women worked in the pits.

TOP: JIMMIE JOHNSON'S PIT CREW MAKES A TIRE CHANGE. *ABOVE:* KYLE PETTY WORKED IN A PIT CREW BEFORE BECOMING A TOP DRIVER.

Chapter One: Fueling Up

What makes the world of NASCAR go around? That's easy. The fuel that powers its race cars. Each drop is precious. Every second that can be saved during refueling matters. When drivers pull into the pits, their crews spring into action. Each crew member has a job. The job of the gas man is to pour gas into the tank.

A gas man must be very strong. The cans used for refueling hold 12 gallons each. That may not seem like much, but each can weighs around 81 pounds when full. Each car holds 17.75 gallons of fuel. When the first can is empty, the gas man reaches for another one. This crew member fills the tank until it begins to overflow. The catch can man catches any fuel that splashes out.

A NASCAR PIT CREW REFUELS A CAR. WHEN THE FIRST CAN IS EMPTY, ANOTHER WILL BE PASSED OVER THE WALL.

In the Mix

The best type of fuel for racing engines has always had a lot of lead. Lead added to gas makes an engine perform better. Unfortunately, leaded fuel is bad for us and the environment. NASCAR tested cleaner fuels for more than thirty years. It finally found one that worked. In 2008, all pit crews started using unleaded fuel for the first time.

TOP: A NASCAR GAS MAN CAN BE A MAN OR A WOMAN. NO MATTER WHAT, THE GAS MAN MUST WEAR SAFETY GEAR FROM HEAD TO TOE. *ABOVE:* PERFECT TIMING IS NEEDED TO REFUEL A CAR AND CHANGE ALL FOUR TIRES QUICKLY.

Powering Up

A NASCAR pit stop is very different from a visit to your neighborhood gas station. The machines that refuel a family car are made to pump the gasoline very slowly. Between 10 and 15 seconds are needed to fill a NASCAR fuel cell (gas tank). The gas stations you see every day can only pump a gallon or two in the same amount of time.

The fuel used in NASCAR races is also different from the gas pumped into a family car. NASCAR fuel has a very high octane level. Octane levels show the amount of energy that different types of fuel can produce. The higher the octane level, the more power a car has. The high-octane NASCAR fuel also keeps engines running smoothly at fast speeds.

KURT BUSCH'S CREW REFUELS HIS CAR
BEFORE A PRACTICE RUN.

Do the Math

Starting in 2008, every car began using fuel cells that held 17.75 gallons. The old tanks held 22.5 gallons. How much less gas do the new fuel cells hold?

(answer on page 48)

Show of Force

Gravity is the name of the force that pulls everything toward the middle of the earth. Gravity keeps cars on the track. It keeps your feet on the ground. NASCAR pit crews depend on gravity to help move fuel from the gas cans to their cars in just a few seconds.

TONY STEWART'S PIT CREW FILLS UP HIS
CAR'S TANK DURING A PIT STOP.

Safety First

The job of a gas man is very dangerous. A stray spark can light racing fuel and create a fire. One gallon of gasoline can explode with the force of 20 sticks of dynamite. So every member of the pit crew is extra careful. The gas man and the catch can man wear protective helmets. Their clothing guards against catching fire.

NASCAR allows only seven people to hop over the pit wall during pit stops. However, other crew members can help them from the other side. Some use long poles to reach over the wall. They might clean track grit and garbage from a car's front grille. They can offer the driver a bottle of water.

DENNY HAMLIN REFUELS AT POCONO RACEWAY IN PENNSYLVANIA.

ABOVE: PIT CREW MEMBERS WHO WORK AROUND FUEL MUST WEAR SAFETY GEAR. *BELOW:* WARD BURTON'S CAR WAS HIT FROM BEHIND. THE FUEL CELL IS BUILT TO SURVIVE ACCIDENTS.

By Design

The fuel cell in a NASCAR vehicle sits behind the driver, under the car's trunk. The fuel cell is made of a strong and flexible rubber container called a bladder. Sturdy steel surrounds the bladder. NASCAR fuel cells are designed for safety. They can even survive high-speed wrecks.

See for Yourself

Look closely at the gas can the next time you watch a NASCAR race. You will see a small valve on top. It controls how much air flows into the can. The valve also manages how fast the fuel pours out. To understand how the valve works, try this experiment.

- Fill a glass to the top with water.
- Put a straw in the water, touching the bottom of the glass. Pinch the top of the straw as hard as you can.
- Lift the straw above the glass. You'll notice the water stays inside the straw.
- Lessen the pressure slightly to allow a tiny bit of air in the top of the straw. The water will trickle out slowly. Count how long it takes for the straw to empty into the glass.
- Refill the straw. But this time, let the air rush in faster. The water empties into the glass faster than you can count!

The gas man has to know exactly how much air to let into the bladder with the fuel.

Save It For Later

LEFT: JUAN PABLO MONTOYA CELEBRATES HIS FIRST NASCAR VICTORY. *BELOW:* MONTOYA TALKS TO DONNIE WINGO *(BELOW LEFT)*.

At the Infineon Raceway in California in 2007, Juan Pablo Montoya was just 20 laps away from his first NASCAR victory. He was in third place. He and his crew chief, Donnie Wingo, had talked many times about the importance of saving fuel. This time, Montoya took Wingo's advice. He did not push his car too hard and use up fuel. At the end of the race, he had just enough fuel to finish. He passed the leaders, who were running out of gas.

Shoptalk

"HE SAVED ENOUGH FUEL TO MAKE IT....WITHOUT THE FUEL MILEAGE, WE'D HAVE NEVER MADE IT."

—CREW CHIEF DONNIE WINGO, ON JUAN PABLO MONTOYA'S FIRST NASCAR VICTORY

When a car pulls into the pits, every second counts. Four members of the seven-person crew are in charge of changing the tires. Their goal is to replace all four tires in under 16 seconds.

The two tire changers carry air wrenches. These tools look like guns with hoses attached. They use the power of air to quickly loosen the five lug nuts that hold each old tire in place. The tire carriers help to put a new tire on the axle. The new tire is already mounted to a wheelbase. Lug nuts are already glued over the holes. This saves precious seconds, because the tire changers only have to tighten the nuts with the air wrench. Each carrier-changer team does the right side tires first. Then they tackle the left side tires.

A TIRE CARRIER HOPS OVER THE PIT WALL AS HIS DRIVER'S CAR COMES IN.

Do the Math

Your two tire-changing crews have 16 seconds to remove and replace four tires. How much time do they spend on each tire?

(answer on page 48)

RIGHT: A MEMBER OF JOE NEMECHEK'S PIT CREW TEACHES A YOUNG FAN HOW TO CHANGE A TIRE. *BELOW:* TIRE CHANGERS QUICKLY ROLL THE LAST TWO TIRES AWAY AFTER A PIT STOP.

Do the Math

The tires used in most races weigh 75 pounds each. During one pit stop, a tire carrier puts on two new tires and takes off two old tires. What is the total amount of weight the tire carrier has handled?

(answer on page 48)

Friction Connection

Tires work by transferring the energy of the engine to the road. The less energy that is wasted, the faster the car will go. The tires used by NASCAR drivers create just the right amount of friction between the rubber and the pavement. Friction describes how two surfaces act when they rub against each other. Too little friction and the tires slip, wasting precious energy. Too much friction and the tires wear down, which also wastes energy.

A NASCAR racing team decides which tires will work best. They can choose from around eighteen different types of rubber blends. Softer tires give more friction and more speed. But they wear down faster. So they will have to be changed more often. Stiffer tires last longer. But they don't give as much friction.

BOBBY LABONTE'S TIRES ARE SLIPPING DURING A TEST RUN. HE NEEDS TIRES WITH MORE FRICTION.

TIRE WEAR IS CHECKED AFTER EVERY
PRACTICE RUN. ONE CREW MEMBER *(BELOW)*
USES A BLOWTORCH. ANOTHER *(RIGHT)*
MARKS PROBLEM SPOTS WITH A PEN.

Do the Math

*During all the phases
of a race weekend, NASCAR
pit crews typically use 12
sets of four tires. The cost of
each tire is $500. How much
is spent on this part of the
car by the end of the race?*

(answer on page 48)

The Pressure's On

During a race, NASCAR pit crews make many slight changes to help their cars run smoothly. One of the most common changes is to the air pressure in the tires. Increasing or decreasing the pressure of each tire makes the car handle a little differently. For example, letting out a tiny bit of air in one tire may fix a small problem a driver feels going through turns.

If there is a bigger problem, a pit crew may decide to change the pressure in all four tires. While a car is on the track, the team figures out how much to raise or lower the tire pressure. The crew then prepares a new set of tires for the next pit stop. This way, the changes don't add time to the pit stops.

A WORKER MOVES STACKS OF TIRES BEFORE A RACE. PIT CREWS HAVE A LOT OF TIRES TO CHOOSE FROM.

ABOVE: IF THERE IS A TIRE PROBLEM DURING A RACE, THE PIT CREW MUST WORK FAST TO SOLVE IT. LEFT: A SPECIALIST CHECKS THE PRESSURE ON TIRES AT THE DAYTONA INTERNATIONAL SPEEDWAY IN FLORIDA.

By Design

Increasing tire pressure makes tires stiffer. Stiffer tires give a car more spring in the suspension system. A greater spring rate helps a car handle the bumps in a race track better.

See for Yourself

During a race, the right side tires travel farther than the left side tires. Is the difference large or small? Try this experiment, and see for yourself.

- Unfold a newspaper on the floor. This is your "track."
- Find a toy car, about the size of your hand.
- Wet the wheels of the car. Quickly guide it around the newspaper in an oval shape. The car should be traveling to the left, like it would at most NASCAR races. You should have made two dark lines.
- Carefully lay a length of string around the outside line. Cut the string with a scissors where the string meets itself.
- Take the string and lay it along the inside line. Notice that the end of the string overlaps the beginning of the string.

The extra part of the string shows how much farther the right tires travel than the left tires on every lap. During a long race, this amount of wear really adds up!

AT FAST TRACKS LIKE
ALABAMA'S TALLADEGA
SUPERSPEEDWAY *(RIGHT)*,
GOOD TIRES CAN MAKE THE
DIFFERENCE BETWEEN
WINNING AND LOSING.

*In 1969, Junior Johnson and LeeRoy Yarbrough
tested the first slicks, or tires without treads (grooves).
Treadless tires gave drivers control at speeds that
treaded tires could not. NASCAR approved the use of
treadless tires right away.*

JUNIOR JOHNSON *(RIGHT)* TALKS WITH
DARRELL WALTRIP IN THE GARAGE.

Shoptalk

"TIRES MAKE THE DIFFERENCE
BETWEEN TENTH AND FIRST—AND
THAT'S A LOT OF DIFFERENCE."

—DRIVER JUNIOR JOHNSON

Chapter Three: Under the Hood

If everything is working right, drivers are usually able to travel about 100 miles before they need more fuel and fresh tires. While they are racing around the track, their pit crews prepare for the next stop. If something is not working as well as it should, the crew must decide quickly how to make it work better.

Experienced pit crews look for ways to help their drivers during a race. Experienced drivers can help their pit crews too. If a car is not handling well, the driver uses the radio to describe the problem to the crew chief. When the car pulls into the pits, the crew makes changes quickly. Everyone on the team knows they only have a few seconds.

RYAN NEWMAN'S PIT CREW WORKS ON HIS ENGINE. NEWMAN RADIOED HIS CREW THAT HIS ENGINE HAD A PROBLEM. THE CREW MEMBERS WERE READY TO FIX IT WHEN HE PULLED IN.

TONY STEWART'S TEAM TALKS ABOUT THEIR PRERACE PLAN.

Do the Math

Car A enters the pits two seconds before Car B. Car A's crew spends seventeen seconds on new tires and refueling. How long does Car B's pit stop have to be to beat Car A back onto the track?

(answer on page 48)

Inside Job

One way to improve the handling of a car during a race is to make a small change to the rear springs. The springs control how much weight is put on each tire. This is important to the balance a driver needs to race at top speeds. The rear tire carrier uses a long socket wrench to increase or decrease the pressure on one of the springs. The carrier makes this adjustment through an opening in the rear window of the car.

JOHN ANDRETTI RESTS HIS FOOT ON A SPRING DURING A BREAK IN THE ACTION. SPRINGS ARE IMPORTANT TO THE HANDLING OF A CAR.

Sometimes during a pit stop, a crew member will put a wrench in an opening near the outside rear tire. This is how the track bar is raised or lowered. The track bar joins the rear axle to the car's frame. The track bar keeps the wheels centered under the car's body. This helps the car stay stable at high speeds

CREW CHIEF DONNIE WINGO USES A LONG-HANDLED TOOL TO MAKE A CHANGE TO A CAR.

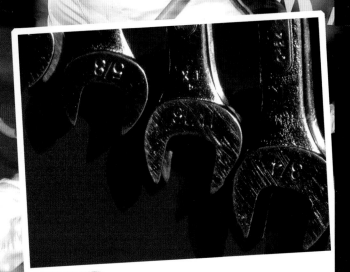

By Design

A socket wrench is designed to turn nuts quickly in tight spaces. A ratchet device on the wrench allows movement in only one direction. The socket size can be changed depending on the size of the nut that has to be turned.

TOP: A TIRE CHANGER MOVES QUICKLY DURING THE NASCAR SPRINT PIT CREW CHALLENGE. SPEED IS EVERYTHING WHEN YOU ARE PART OF A PIT CREW. *ABOVE:* A NASCAR CREW HAS EVERY SIZE AND LENGTH OF WRENCH.

Timing Is Everything

Not every pit stop is the same. Changing all four tires and refueling a near-empty tank usually takes fifteen to sixteen seconds. In the mad dash to beat other drivers back onto the track, a crew chief may decide to save time. The crew may replace only the tires on the right side. Near the end of a race, a driver may only get enough fuel to make it to the finish line. And the team may leave on all the old tires. This type of pit stop is called a "splash and go." It only takes a few seconds.

ELLIOTT SADLER'S TEAM LOOKS AT DAMAGE TO SADLER'S CAR DURING A PIT STOP. THEY ONLY HAVE A FEW SECONDS TO REPAIR IT.

CLINT BOWYER DRIVES HIS CAR TOWARD THE GARAGE AREA TO GET IT FIXED.

Sometimes a bad problem happens during a race. A car may be damaged in an accident. The engine may not work properly. Part of the suspension system, which helps the car ride smoothly, may be broken. Or fluids may be leaking out of the car. In these cases, a driver will steer the car to a safe area behind the pit wall where repairs can be made. This type of stop can take several minutes. This much time can put a driver in last place.

In the Mix

When a car takes on fuel near the end of a race, the crew puts in only what the driver needs to finish. A gallon of racing fuel weighs around 7 pounds. (A gallon of water weighs about 8 pounds.) Still, even one extra gallon can slow down a driver enough to lose a race.

See for Yourself

How quickly do NASCAR pit crews have to work? To get an idea, try this experiment on a parked car. Make sure you are in a safe area, such as a driveway, with no traffic. You will need a stopwatch or a friend to keep time.

- Mark a spot on the ground that is about 10 feet away from the left side of the car. This will be your start and finish line.
- Start the clock (or start counting), and move quickly to the right front tire.
- Use a stick to touch five different places on the wheel, in a star pattern.
- Touch the same five places again on the same wheel.
- Move to the left front tire and repeat this work.
- Run back to the start/finish line, and check your time.

Imagine having to do that with an air wrench while changing two tires!

Colorful Crew

JEFF GORDON'S CREW ROLLS OUT HIS CAR FOR A PRACTICE RUN.

Jeff Gordon has one of the most famous NASCAR pit crews. His team helped him win four NASCAR Sprint Cup Series championships between 1995 and 2001. The crew members were called the Rainbow Warriors for their brightly colored uniforms.

Shoptalk

"I WANT THIS TEAM TO FEEL LIKE A UNIT, LIKE A FAMILY."

—DRIVER JEFF GORDON, ON HIS RACING TEAM

FOR JEFF GORDON, EVERY CREW MEMBER IS LIKE A MEMBER OF HIS FAMILY.

Chapter Four: Making the Team

Each NASCAR pit crew is put together differently. In most cases, team members do another job in the days before a race. The front tire changer, for example, may work on the suspension system. The jack man may be a mechanic. The gas man may drive one of the team's support vehicles. What all pit crew members have in common is that they are quick and strong. They must stay in great shape so that no time is wasted during pit stops. Some crews hire people just to work at a race. Crew chiefs have tryouts to see who is the strongest and the fastest. Even former college and professional athletes try out. Special schools teach the skills needed to work in the pits.

A NASCAR TEAM NEEDS TO BE STRONG AND QUICK IN THE PITS AND IN THE GARAGE TOO.

Do the Math

The weight of a driver adds to the total weight of a car. One of the lightest drivers in NASCAR is Kurt Busch. He weighs about 155 pounds. One of the heaviest is Jimmy Spencer. He tips the scales at 225 pounds. What is the difference in their weights?

(answer on page 48)

Shoptalk

"[CREW MEMBERS] RUN, LIFT WEIGHTS,...WORK ON FOOT SPEED.... EVERYTHING IS MEASURED NOT JUST IN TENTHS [OF SECONDS], BUT IN THOUSANDTHS OF SECONDS."

—JEFF HAMMOND, CO-OWNER OF PIT INSTRUCTION AND TRAINING

ATHLETES CAN SHARPEN THEIR SKILLS BY WORKING ON CARS *(TOP)* AND BY LISTENING TO DRIVERS AND CREW CHIEFS *(ABOVE).*

Two for the Show

A pit crew has four people who work on the tires. One person refuels the car. Another catches fuel splashes. The last crew member who leaps over the wall is the jack man.

JUAN PABLO MONTOYA'S PIT CREW SPRINGS INTO ACTION.

The jack man's job is to lift the car off the ground so that the tire changers can work. This crew member uses a hydraulic jack to raise the car. The 3,400-pound car must go up with just a couple of pumps on each side. The right side tires are changed first. Then the jack man jacks up the left side. When the left side is done, the jack man lowers the jack. The jack man signals the driver that the car is good to go.

ABOVE: WARD BURTON'S PIT CREW IS ABOUT TO FINISH A TIRE CHANGE. *LEFT:* MATT KENSETH'S JACK MAN RAISES HIS CAR WITH JUST A FEW PUMPS. *BELOW LEFT:* A NEW TIRE IS TRADED FOR A WORN ONE DURING A PIT STOP BY RYAN NEWMAN.

Do the Math

A good jack man can get a car off the ground in two pumps. This happens twice during a tire change. Let's say a car changes tires six times during the race. How many pumps does the jack man make in all?

(answer on page 48)

Working Out

Most NASCAR pit crews have a coach. The coach watches the crew members during pit stops and gives them advice on how to be quicker or better. In between pit stops, the coach keeps the team focused and energized so they are ready to leap over the wall. Between races, the pit coach makes sure crew members are in good shape. They practice working together as a team.

Racing fans have favorite drivers and cars. They also have favorite crews. In May of 2005, NASCAR held the first NASCAR Sprint Pit Crew Challenge. The event tested the speed and skill of the top teams. Kurt Busch's crew won the competition. The seven-member team divided the $100,000 prize.

TWO CREWS COMPETE SIDE BY SIDE DURING THE 2007 NASCAR SPRINT PIT CREW CHALLENGE.

By Design

When the pits are crowded with cars, a driver may have trouble finding the correct pit box. A crew member holds a sign with the driver's car number on it. Sometimes the crew chief talks to the driver on the radio. The chief counts down—three, two, one—so the driver knows how close the pit crew is.

TOP: THE REAL VICTORIES COME ON THE TRACKS. MATT KENSETH'S CREW JUMPS FOR JOY AFTER HE CROSSES THE FINISH LINE. ABOVE: THE PITS CAN GET VERY CROWDED DURING A RACE!

See for Yourself

Why do NASCAR pit crews work out between races? Because the harder they train, the better they perform. See for yourself by making a chart with seven columns. Write today's date and the day of the week at the top of the first column. Put the other dates and days of the week in the next six columns.

- Set a kitchen timer to one minute.
- Start the timer. Count how many push-ups you can do in a minute.
- Each time you touch the floor with your chest and then straighten your arms counts as one push-up.
- Mark down the number of push-ups you were able to do in the first column.
- Repeat this experiment each day for a week. Try to do the exercise around the same time each day.

At the end of the week, you should be able to do a few more push-ups in a minute than you could at the beginning of the week. This is because your muscles are getting stronger. Each push-up is happening faster too. The increased speed that comes with strength is why NASCAR pit crew members work out.

Perfect Fit

In 1992, Ray Evernham decided to make the members of his pit crew into better athletes. He and Andy Papathanassiou, a former football player, came up with special workouts and training. Other pit crews laughed at them. But the hard work paid off. Evernham's young driver, Jeff Gordon, became the NASCAR Sprint Cup Series champion just three years later.

Shoptalk

"WHEN ONE TEAM BRINGS IN AN EX-NFL PLAYER, AND THAT PERSON IS TWO STEPS QUICKER THAN EVERYBODY ELSE, NOW YOU'VE [RAISED] THE BAR FOR EVERYBODY."

—BREON KLOPP, DIRECTOR OF PIT INSTRUCTION AND TRAINING

RAY EVERNHAM CHANGED THE WAY PIT CREWS WORK AND TRAIN.

Chapter Five: Who's the Boss?

All of the people on NASCAR teams have important jobs to do on race day. Drivers must compete with one another. Pit crews must get their cars back on the track as quickly as possible. Behind the pit wall, other team members talk about ways to improve the performance of their cars, their drivers, and their pit crews. The person responsible for making final decisions is the crew chief.

A CREW CHIEF WATCHES PIT STOPS LIKE THIS
ONE AND LOOKS FOR WAYS TO SAVE TIME.

The crew chief decides on a team's strategy—both on the track and in the pits. The mind of a crew chief devours information during a race. This team leader needs to know everything about the car and the driver. The crew chief must also know as much as possible about the other cars and drivers. The crew chief must be familiar with the track too.

LEFT: THE DECISIONS OF A CREW CHIEF CAN MAKE THE DIFFERENCE IN A CLOSE RACE LIKE THIS ONE. *BELOW LEFT:* JIMMIE JOHNSON *(LEFT)* DISCUSSES STRATEGY WITH HIS CREW CHIEF, CHAD KNAUS.

Do the Math

When the pit crew members hop over the wall, they are carrying heavy equipment. They have two 75-pound tires, two 81-pound gas cans, two 5-pound air wrenches, and a 30-pound jack. What is the total weight they are carrying?

(answer on page 48)

Calling the Shots

The crew chief is in charge of preparing the team's car for a race. Once the race begins, the crew chief is like the manager of a baseball team. If the team's car is the fastest on the track, the crew chief makes sure that the car doesn't lose time during the race. If the team's car isn't the fastest, the crew chief tries to plan the pit stops perfectly. The crew chief tells the driver when to be patient and when to pass. At the end of a race, the first person a winning driver thanks is usually the crew chief. And the crew chief deserves it!

BETWEEN PIT STOPS, CREW CHIEFS SOMETIMES WATCH THE RACE ON TV SCREENS. BRIAN PATTIE (RIGHT) AND A CREW MEMBER WATCH THEIR DRIVER AT THE RICHMOND INTERNATIONAL RACEWAY IN VIRGINIA.

Crew chiefs are always in contact with their drivers on the radio. Some talk a lot. Some talk a little. The only thing a crew chief cannot tell a driver is what's happening around the track. That is the job of a spotter. This person watches the race from high above the grandstand. The spotter is also in direct contact with the driver. The spotter warns the driver of accidents and encourages the driver during a race.

TWO NASCAR CREW CHIEFS TALK TO THEIR DRIVERS. GREG ERWIN (*LEFT*) AND DOUG RICHERT (*BELOW LEFT*) DEPEND ON THEIR RADIOS TO STAY IN CONTACT.

Do the Math

A poor pit stop has pushed the first-place car six seconds off the lead. The car makes three more pit stops before the end of the race. How much time does the pit crew need to make up at each stop to catch up?

(answer on page 48)

Rules, Rules, Rules

A crew chief must be an expert when it comes to the rules. NASCAR has a lot of rules. They are put in place to improve safety. They make sure that no driver has an unfair advantage. For example, all drivers must slow down when entering the pits. On some tracks, the speed limit may be as low as 35 miles per hour.

When a driver stops in the pits, the car must be within the boundaries of the pit box. The tire changers cannot allow an old tire to roll outside the pit box. All the lug nuts on the tires must be tightened before a car may leave the pits. All equipment, including the hydraulic jack and air wrenches, must be taken back over the wall.

A RACE AT THE TEXAS MOTOR SPEEDWAY IN FORT WORTH IS ABOUT TO BEGIN. NASCAR TEAMS MUST FOLLOW THE RULES BEFORE, DURING, AND AFTER EACH RACE.

A NASCAR OFFICIAL TELLS ELLIOTT SADLER'S CREW
THAT HE HAS STOPPED OUTSIDE OF THE PIT BOX.

By Design

NASCAR drivers don't
have speedometers to tell
them how fast they are
going. Instead, they use
tachometers. These devices
tell them how hard their
engines are working. At the
beginning of each race, all
the cars run a pace lap at
the maximum speed allowed
on pit road. Drivers must
remember this tachometer
reading. They slow down to
this reading on their way
into the pits during the race.

See for Yourself

NASCAR crew chiefs must do a lot of mental juggling during a race. How good a juggler of information are you? Try this experiment.

- Ask five friends to pick one small object each—a coin or eraser or key, for example.
- With your friends standing in a line, look at the objects. Then have them close their hands tightly, covering the objects.
- Ask each friend to quiz you with a simple math problem. For example, 9 plus 2 or 20 minus 12.
- Have your friends switch places in line.
- Ask each of them to give you a slightly harder math problem. For example, 3 plus 3 times 3.
- Can you remember what was in each friend's hand?

Why Do It?

The job of crew chief might be one of the hardest in all of sports. A crew chief works twice as many hours as most people do. The crew chief takes the blame when a team doesn't win. The driver gets most of the glory after a victory. And every season, the job gets more involved. Why would anyone want to be a crew chief? Because it's also the coolest job on pit road!

CREW CHIEF STEVE LETARTE *(LEFT)* AND DRIVER JEFF GORDON TALK ABOUT THEIR CAR'S ENGINE. THE CREW CHIEF AND DRIVER MUST WORK TOGETHER WELL TO WIN RACES.

Shoptalk

"THE JOB OF THE CREW CHIEF IS ALMOST TOO BIG FOR ONE PERSON."

—RAY EVERNHAM,
JEFF GORDON'S CREW CHIEF
DURING THE 1990s

DRIVER CASEY MEARS *(LEFT)* AND CREW CHIEF DARIAN GRUBB PLAN THEIR PRACTICE RUNS AT THE CALIFORNIA SPEEDWAY.

Glossary

bladder: the flexible container that holds the gas in a race car's gas tank

catch can man: the pit crew member who uses a container to catch overflowing gas during refueling

friction: the effect of two surfaces rubbing against each other

gas man: the pit crew member who refuels a race car's gas tank

hydraulics: the science that compresses (squeezes) liquid to make power

jack man: the pit crew member who raises the race car, one side at a time, to let the tires be changed

lap: one circuit around a track; to be ahead of another car by one entire circuit of the track

lug nut: a rounded bolt cover that attaches a wheel to an axle

NASCAR: the National Association for Stock Car Auto Racing

passing: going by a moving car to get in front of it

pit box: a marked-off area where each team can service its race car

pit crew: during a race the seven-member team that takes care of a race car during a race. The crew chief leads the pit crew.

suspension system: the springs, shocks, and other parts that are used to suspend (hang) a car's frame, body, and engine above the wheels

tachometer: a device that measures how many engine revolutions happen per minute

tire carrier: the pit crew member who brings the new tires to the pitbox and takes away old tires

tire changer: the pit crew member who removes and replaces tires during a pit stop

valve: a device that controls the flow of a liquid or gas

Learn More

Books

Buckley, James.   *NASCAR*. New York: DK Eyewitness Books, 2005.

Buckley, James.   *Speedway Superstars*. Pleasantville, NY: Reader's Digest, 2004.

Doeden, Matt.   *Stock Cars*. Minneapolis: Lerner Publications Company, 2007.

Fielden, Greg.   *NASCAR Chronicle*. Lincolnwood, IL: Publications International, Ltd., 2003.

Sporting News.   *NASCAR Record & Fact Book*. Charlotte, NC: Sporting News, 2007.

Woods, Bob.   *The Greatest Races*. Pleasantville, NY: Reader's Digest, 2004.

Woods, Bob.   *NASCAR Pit Pass: Behind the Scenes of NASCAR*. Pleasantville, NY: Reader's Digest, 2005.

Website and Video Game

NASCAR
http://www.nascar.com
NASCAR.com is the official site of NASCAR.
From here you can find information on drivers and their teams, as well as previews of upcoming races, schedules, and a look back at NASCAR's history.

NASCAR 2008. Video game. Redwood City, CA: EA Sports, 2008.
With an ESRB rating of E for "everyone," this game gives fans a chance to experience the speed and thrills of driving in a NASCAR race.

Index

Do the Math Answers

Page 8: 4.75 gallons. 22.5 gallons − 17.75 gallons = 4.75 gallons.

Page 14: 8 seconds. 16 seconds ÷ 2 crews = 8 seconds per crew.

Page 15: 300 pounds. 4 tires x 75 pounds = 300 pounds.

Page 17: $24,000. $500 x 4 tires = $2,000 per set x 12 sets = $24,000.

Page 23: 14 seconds. 17 seconds − 2 seconds = 15 seconds to match Car A's time − 1 second to beat Car A's time = 14 seconds.

Page 31: 70 pounds. 225 pounds − 155 pounds = 70 pounds.

Page 33: 24 pumps. 2 pumps x 2 sides = 4 pumps per pit stop x 6 pit stops = 24 pumps.

Page 39: 352 pounds. 75 + 75 + 81 + 81 + 5 + 5 + 30 = 352 pounds.

Page 41: 2 seconds. 6 seconds ÷ 3 pits stops = 2 seconds per pit stop.